We the People

domestic Tranquility provide for the common

P...

D0736062

_____

to

_____

by

_____

date

_____

in Honor of my Hero

We the People

insure domestic Tranquility, provide for the common ...
and our Posterity, do ordain and establish this Constitu...

Section. 1. All legislative Powers herein granted shal...
of Representatives.

Section. 2. The House of Representatives shall be comp...
in each State shall have the Qualifications requisite for Electors of th...

No Person shall be a Representative who shall not ha...
and who shall not, when elected, be an Inhabitant of that State...

Representatives and direct Taxes shall be apportioned am...
Numbers, which shall be determined by adding to the whole Nu...
not taxed, three fifths of all other Persons. The actual Enumer...
and within...

IN
God
WE **STILL**
TRUST

DR. RICHARD G. LEE

THOMAS NELSON
Since 1798

NASHVILLE DALLAS MEXICO CITY RIO DE JANEIRO BEIJING

Contents

Introduction 7

A Call to Action 8

First Prayer in Congress 10

Faith of the Founders 12

Christianity in Colonial
America 15

The Liberty Bell 19

"God Bless America" 20

John Glenn 21

National Blessing 22

Communion on the Moon 23

Common Sense 24

American Bible Society 25

Eternal Vigilance 26

The First Book Published in the
American Colonies 27

Religion and Morality 28

The Bible of the Revolution 29

Samuel Morse 30

"Without God" 31

"Let's Roll!" 32

"I Am an American" 33

Staying True to the Christian
Religion 34

How to Be Successful 35

A Policeman's Prayer 36

A Legacy of Success 37

Government Paid Legislative
Chaplains 38

The "Holy Experiment" 39

The Cornerstone of American
Society 40

Boston Tea Party 41

Good Works 42

George Washington's "Earnest
Prayer" 43

On Civil Liberty 44

Duty—Honor—Country 45

Shield of Strength 46

The Northwest Ordinance 47

"The American Sound" 48

The Foundation of America 49

The Use of Power 50

Life and Immortality 51

Francis Marion, the "Swamp
Fox" 52

The Fourth of July Celebration . . 53

True History or Consummate
Fraud? 54

The First National Day of
Thanksgiving 55

The Designer of the Universe . . 56

Man as God's Coworker 57

Patriotism 58

The Government and Nativity
Scenes 59

Fill the World with His Glory . . . 60

"God, Give Us Men" 61

Defending the Unborn 62

Correcting Abuses 63

Days of Fasting 64

Christian Men of Science 65

"Sail On, O Ship of State!" 66

Rules of Moral Action 67

The Land of the Bible 68

Facing Fear in Dark Hours 69

A Fireman's Prayer 70

"Duty to God" 71

Who but the Ruler of the
   Winds? 72

The Last Bastion of Freedom . . . 73

In Defense of Life 74

The Bible's Influence on the
   Founding Fathers 75

True Christian, True Citizen 76

Yes, There Is Hope 77

Christianity and Common Law . . 78

Purpose of a Public Education . . 79

A Wise and Frugal Government . . 80

Render Honor to the Creator . . . 81

"I Was Free" 82

The General Principles of
   Liberty 83

The Purifying Influence of
   Christianity 84

No Book Like the Bible 85

"The Destiny of America" 86

The Haystack Prayer Meeting . . . 87

"The God Who Made the
   Peanut" 88

The Purest Morality 89

No Ordinary Claims 90

Religion Supports the State 91

"The Battle Hymn of the
   Republic" 92

"My Country, 'Tis of Thee" 94

Introduction

WHILE OTHER NATIONS have built their governments upon the shaky foundations of communism, socialism, and countless other anti-God philosophies, only to see those foundations crumble, America stands without equal as a beacon of hope and freedom in a hurting world. Our Founding Fathers delivered to us a system of government that has enjoyed unprecedented success: we are now the world's longest ongoing constitutional republic. Well over two hundred years under one form of government is an accomplishment unknown among contemporary nations.

Within this special edition of *In God We Still Trust,* you will find a great volume of both information and inspiration revealing the "strong cord" of the Bible's influence that runs through the colorful fabric of our nation's past and present.

Much effort has gone into the verification of the quotes and stories included so that the reader can be assured of the validity of that which is recorded herein. To handle the Word of God in any manner is to do so with great care and respect, and that has been done by all who have been involved in this project. May God bless the truth within these pages, and may God continue to bless America!

Dr. Richard G. Lee

A Call to Action

WHILE WE HAVE MUCH to admire and love and be thankful for in being able to call America our home, our nation is rapidly drifting from its biblical foundations. Our freedom to serve God and to promote the gospel in our land is disintegrating. We are engaged in a great spiritual battle that threatens our country, our families, and our lives. Only God's intervention will return America to solid footing and restore a moral nation that righteousness will exalt.

As believers in Jesus, we have His call to be "salt" and "light" to the world (Matthew 5:13–16). We must take seriously our responsibility to put God first, not only in our homes but also in our national affairs.

Pray. Our Founding Fathers knew the power and purpose of prayer. From our nation's beginning through times of war and tragedy, we have been called to pray that the hand of Almighty God might show forth His mercy and intervene with His grace toward America. Today is no different. Second Chronicles 7:14 instructs us: *". . . if My people who are called by My name will humble themselves, and pray and seek My face, and turn from their wicked ways, then I will hear from heaven, and will forgive their sin and heal their land."*

Process. Within the God-given wisdom of our founding documents, we have been granted clear and certain processes for bringing about change concerning things that we perceive as wrong for our land. From the local municipality to the halls of Congress and the White House, imbedded in the laws and governmental processes of America are pathways for non-violent moral, social, and political change. But first they must be learned and understood before they can be properly applied.

Participate. Participating within the process for change is the ultimate key to its success. It is futile to gripe and complain about what one considers "wrong" or "unjust" in our land and not participate in the process of changing it for the better. The Scriptures are clear on this matter, "*. . . to him who knows to do good and does not do it, to him it is sin*" (James 4:17).

Persevere. When fighting for the right, we must never cease until we prevail. The battle is not always won by the strongest, the smartest, or the most elite, but ultimately it comes to those who persist and persevere. When soon-to-be President George Washington led his troops into battle during the Revolutionary War, he lost most of those battles, but through perseverance he ultimately won the war. As a result, we won our independence from the British and became a free people. Our Lord taught us that when we put our hands to the plow of a righteous cause, we are never to look back, but to persevere and prevail (Luke 9:62).

FIRST
Prayer
of CONGRESS

OLORD OUR HEAVENLY FATHER, high and mighty King of kings, and Lord of lords, who dost from Thy throne behold all the dwellers on earth and reignest with power supreme and uncontolled over all the kingdoms, empires and governments; look down in mercy, we beseech Thee, on these our American States, who have fled to Thee from the rod of the oppressor and thrown themselves on Thy gracious protection, desiring to be henceforth dependent only on Thee. To Thee have they appealed for the righteousness of their cause; to Thee do they now look up for that countenance and support, which Thou alone canst give. Take them, therefore, Heavenly Father, under Thy nurturing care; give them wisdom in council and valor in the field; defeat the malicious designs of our cruel adversaries; convince them of the unrighteousness of their cause and if they persist in their sanguinary purposes, of own unerring justice, sounding in their hearts, constrain them to drop the weapons of war from their unnerved bands in the day of battle!

Be Thou present, 0 God of wisdom, and direct the councils of this honroable assembly; enable them to settle things on the best and surest foundation. That the scene of blood may be speedily closed; that order, harmony, and peace may be effectually restored, and truth and justice, religion and piety, prevail and flourish amongst the people. Preserve the health of their bodies and vigor of their minds; shower down on them and the millions they here represent, such temporal blessings as Thou seest expedient for them in this world and crown them with everlasting glory in the world to come. All this we ask in the name and through the merits of Jesus Christ, Thy Son and our Savior. Amen.

—The First Prayer offerred in Congress,
September 7, 1774 by Jacob Duche

Faith of the Founders

W HILE MUCH HAS BEEN written in recent years
to try to dismiss the fact that America was
founded upon the biblical principles of Judeo-
Christianity, all the revisionism in the world cannot change
the facts. Anyone who examines the original writings, personal correspondence, biographies, and public statements
of the individuals who were instrumental in the founding
of America will find an abundance of quotations showing
the profound extent to which their thinking and lives were
influenced by a Christian worldview.

Clearly, there was a predominant Christian consensus in
colonial America that shaped the Founders' thinking and
their writing of the founding documents and laws, resulting in the republic we have today. The Declaration of Independence identified the source of all authority and rights as

"Their Creator," and then accentuated that individual human rights were God-given, not man-made. Thus, there would be no king or established religion to stand in the way of human liberty or dignity—uniquely Judeo-Christian ideals.

Even a brief study of the Founders' last wills and testaments provides convincing declarations of the strong religious beliefs among so many of them. Add to that their personal writings concerning their faith in Christ, plus their leadership roles in establishing and guiding numerous Bible societies, plus their service in active ministries, and the evidence is overwhelming.

Here is a small sample
of the convictions of some of the Founders:

Principally and first of all, I give and recommend my soul into the hands of God that gave it: and my body I recommend to the earth ... nothing doubting but at the general resurrection I shall receive the same again by the mercy and power of God.

JOHN HANCOCK | SIGNER OF THE DECLARATION OF INDEPENDENCE

It cannot be emphasized too clearly and too often that this nation was founded, not by religionists, but by Christians; not on religion, but on the gospel of Jesus Christ.

Attributed to PATRICK HENRY

| GOVERNOR OF VIRGINIA

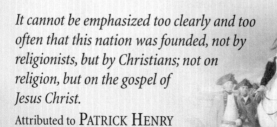

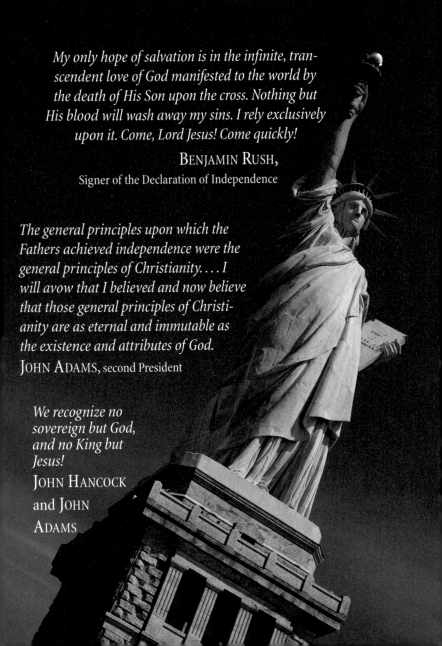

My only hope of salvation is in the infinite, transcendent love of God manifested to the world by the death of His Son upon the cross. Nothing but His blood will wash away my sins. I rely exclusively upon it. Come, Lord Jesus! Come quickly!

BENJAMIN RUSH,
Signer of the Declaration of Independence

The general principles upon which the Fathers achieved independence were the general principles of Christianity. . . . I will avow that I believed and now believe that those general principles of Christianity are as eternal and immutable as the existence and attributes of God.

JOHN ADAMS, second President

We recognize no sovereign but God, and no King but Jesus!

JOHN HANCOCK and JOHN ADAMS

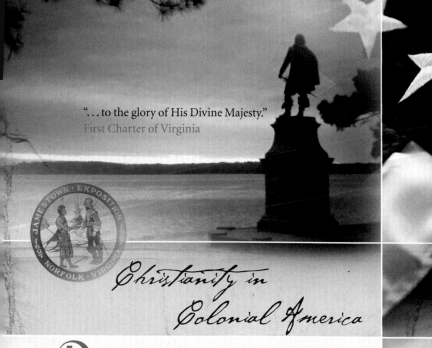

Christianity in Colonial America

BEGINNING EARLY IN THE SEVENTEENTH CENTURY, settlers from Spain, France, Sweden, Holland, and England claimed land and formed colonies along the eastern coast of North America, and the struggle for control of this land continued for well over a hundred years. By the time the Declaration of Independence was signed in 1776, there were thirteen fully operational American colonies with independent governments and constitutions.

The first permanent settlement was the English colony at Jamestown, in 1607, in what is now Virginia. Similar to the other colonial charters, the First Charter of Virginia emphasized the Christian character of their purpose: "We, greatly commending, and graciously accepting of, their desires for the furtherance of so noble a work, which may, by the providence of Almighty God, hereafter tend to the glory of His Divine Majesty, in propagating of Christian religion

15

to such people, as yet live in darkness and miserable ignorance of the true knowledge and worship of God."

In 1620, the Pilgrims followed and set up a colony at Plymouth, in what is now Massachusetts. The purpose of the Pilgrims was to establish a political commonwealth governed by biblical standards. The Mayflower Compact, their initial governing document, clearly stated that what they had undertaken was for "the glory of God and the advancement of the Christian faith." William Bradford, the second governor of Plymouth, said, "[The colonists] cherished a great hope and inward zeal of laying good foundations . . . for the propagations and advance of the Gospel of the kingdom of Christ in the remote parts of the world."

In 1638, a colony was established in New Haven, in what is now Connecticut, by the Reverend John Davenport and Theophilus Eaton. A year later, the Fundamental Orders of Connecticut, often called the world's first written constitution,

was adopted. It reads in part: "For as much as it hath pleased Almighty God by the wise disposition of His Divine Providence so to order and dispose of things that we the inhabitants and residents . . . ; and well knowing where a people are gathered together the Word of God requires that to maintain the peace and union of such a people there should be an orderly and decent government established according to God, to order and dispose of the affairs of the people at all seasons as occasion shall require."

When these colonial settlers arrived in America, the influence of the Bible on their lives came with them. For many, their Christian faith was as much a part of who they were as their brave spirit, and it touched all they touched. This stands out boldly as one sees the goal of government based on Scripture being affirmed over and over by individual colonies, such as in the Rhode Island Charter of 1683, which begins: "We submit our person, lives, and estates unto our Lord Jesus Christ, the King of kings and Lord of lords, and to all those perfect and most absolute laws of His given us in His Holy Word."

From the first colony at Jamestown to the Pennsylvania Charter of Privileges granted to William Penn in 1701, where "all persons who . . . profess to believe in Jesus Christ, the Savior of the world, shall be capable . . . to serve this government in any capacity, both legislatively and executively," the Bible was used as the rule of life in the colonies. Every evidence indicates the profound effect God's Word had on the early Americans.

> "We submit our person, lives, and estates unto our Lord Jesus Christ, the King of kings and Lord of lords, and to all those perfect and most absolute laws of His given us in His Holy Word."
>
> RHODE ISLAND CHARTER OF 1683

WE AUGHT
TO OBEY GOD
RATHER
THAN MEN
(Acts 5:29)

THE LIBERTY BELL

"... proclaim liberty throughout all the land ..."

LEVITICUS 25:10

The Pennsylvania Assembly ordered the bell in 1751 to commemorate the golden anniversary of William Penn's 1701 Charter of Privileges, Pennsylvania's original Constitution, which speaks of the rights and freedoms valued by people the world over. As the bell was created, the biblical quotation "Proclaim liberty throughout all the land unto all the inhabitants thereof" was particularly apt. For the line in the Bible immediately preceding "proclaim liberty" is, "And ye shall hallow the fiftieth year." What better way to pay homage to Penn and hallow the fiftieth year than with a bell proclaiming liberty?

The Liberty Bell gained iconic importance when abolitionists in their efforts to put an end to slavery throughout America adopted it as a symbol of emancipation and liberty in 1837.

Related to a popular fictional story written in 1747, tradition says that on July 8, 1776, the Liberty Bell rang out from the tower of Independence Hall, summoning the citizens of Philadelphia to hear the first public reading of the Declaration of Independence. The truth is that the steeple was in bad condition, and historians today highly doubt this account. However, its association with the Declaration of Independence became fixed in the collective mythology.

19

PRAYER

"GOD BLESS AMERICA"

Born in a poor Russian Jewish ghetto, Irving Berlin immigrated to America with his parents when he was five, settling in New York's Lower East Side. He became one of the most prolific American songwriters in history. "God Bless America" is an American patriotic song he originally wrote in 1918 and revised in 1938, as war and the Nazis were threatening Europe. It takes the form of a prayer for God's blessing and peace for the nation. Singer Kate Smith introduced the revised "God Bless America" during her radio broadcast on Armistice Day 1938, and the song was an immediate sensation. It is considered an unofficial national anthem of the United States.

Irving Berlin

While the storm clouds gather far across the sea,
Let us swear allegiance to a land that's free,
Let us all be grateful for a land so fair,
As we raise our voices in a solemn prayer.

God bless America, land that I love
Stand beside her and guide her
Through the night with the light from above
From the mountains, to the prairies,
to the ocean white with foam
God bless America, my home sweet home.

JOHN GLENN

Between 1957 and 1975, the competition of space exploration between the Soviet Union and the United States became a heated part of the Cold War, both because of its potential military and technological applications and its morale-boosting social benefits. The Soviets were the first to achieve a manned orbit of the earth in 1961, putting America behind in the "Space Race."

On February 20, 1962, atop an Atlas rocket, Colonel John Glenn piloted the first American manned orbital mission aboard Friendship 7, circling the globe three times. Fulfilling America's political and scientific hopes and dreams as declared by President John F. Kennedy, Glenn returned to Earth as virtually every American's hero.

From 1974 to 1999, he served as a United States senator. In 1998, NASA invited him to rejoin the space program as a member of the Space Shuttle Discovery Crew. On October 29, 1998, Glenn became the oldest human, at the age of 77, ever to venture into space. It was a vivid reminder of the heroic spirit that makes space exploration possible.

As Glenn observed the heavens and earth from the windows of Discovery, he said, "To look out at this kind of creation out here and not believe in God is to me impossible. It just strengthens my faith. I wish there were words to describe what it's like."

John Glenn

21

HUMILITY

NATIONAL BLESSING

"Is this not the fast that I have chosen: to loose the bonds of wickedness . . ."

ISAIAH 58:6

Abraham Lincoln, anguished by the ravages of civil war, declared a "Proclamation of a National Fast Day" on March 30, 1863:

Whereas it is the duty of nations as well as of men to own their dependence upon the overruling power of God, to confess their sins and transgressions in humble sorrow, yet with assured hope that genuine repentance will lead to mercy and pardon, and to recognize the sublime truth, announced in the Holy Scriptures and proven by all history, that those nations only are blessed whose God is the Lord.

. . . We have been the recipients of the choicest bounties of Heaven; we have been preserved these many years in peace and prosperity; we have grown in numbers, wealth, and power as no other nation has ever grown. But we have forgotten God. We have forgotten the gracious hand which preserved us in peace and multiplied and enriched and strengthened us, and we have vainly imagined, in the deceitfulness of our hearts, that all these blessings were produced by some superior wisdom and virtue of our own. Intoxicated with unbroken success, we have become too self-sufficient to feel the necessity of redeeming and preserving grace, too proud to pray to the God that made us.

It behooves us, then, to humble ourselves before the offended Power, to confess our national sins, and to pray for clemency and forgiveness.

Abraham Lincoln

COMMUNION ON THE MOON

"I am the vine . . ."
JOHN 15:5

As the Lunar Module pilot on the Apollo 11 space mission, with the first lunar landing on July 20, 1969, Buzz Aldrin was the second person to walk on the moon, after Mission Commander Neil Armstrong. Aldrin had brought with him a tiny communion kit, given him by his church. During the morning, he radioed, "Houston, this is Eagle. . . . I would like to request a few moments of silence. I would like to invite each person listening in . . . to contemplate for a moment the events of the last few hours, and to give thanks in his own individual way."

During the radio blackout, Aldrin took the communion elements and read John 15:5: "I am the vine, you are the branches. He who abides in Me, and I in him, bears much fruit." Aldrin had been asked not to read the verse publicly because of a legal challenge NASA faced from famed atheist Madalyn Murray O'Hair regarding the reading of the biblical creation story from Genesis during the Apollo 8 mission.

How incredible is it that the first thing this American patriot did when he arrived on the moon was to worship God?

Buzz Aldrin

23

DEFENDER

The LORD reigns; let the peoples tremble!

PSALM 99:1

COMMON SENSE BY THOMAS PAINE

In early 1776, Americans still hoped for reconciliation with Britain, and the British were preparing to take advantage of that sentiment with a generous offer for peace that many Americans would have welcomed. But then Thomas Paine anonymously published the political pamphlet *Common Sense* in January 1776, which presented the American colonists with a convincing argument for independence from British rule that resonated with the colonists. In the first year alone, over five hundred thousand copies were sold, and the revolution caught fire.

Paine structured *Common Sense* like a sermon and relied on biblical references and allusions, such as, "But where says some is the king of America? I'll tell you, friend, He reigns above," to make his case to the people. His vision stirred the colonists to strengthen their resolve. By spring 1776, there was significant support for American independence, and Virginia's convention voted to instruct their delegates to Congress to propose that the colonies formally declare their independence. On June 7, Richard Henry Lee moved that Congress declare the United Colonies to be free and independent, resulting in the first successful anticolonial action in modern history.

Thomas Paine

AMERICAN BIBLE SOCIETY

Elias Boudinot Jr. (1740–1821) was an early American lawyer and statesman from Elizabeth, New Jersey. As an energetic patriot, he was elected as a delegate to the Continental Congress from 1777 to 1784, serving as its president from 1782 until 1783. He then served three terms in Congress, followed by the appointment to be the Director of the Mint for ten years. Boudinot supported many civic and educational causes during his life, including serving as one of Princeton's trustees for nearly half a century.

Boudinot was elected president of the American Bible Society at its founding in 1816 and served until his death in 1821. In his letter accepting the office of president, he stated that this was "the greatest honor" that could have been conferred upon him "on this side of the grave." He had an unwavering faith that God had called the men of the society to the work of making Bibles available in America. His ten thousand dollar gift, at a time when an annual salary of $400 was considered good, essentially enabled the formation and early organization of the American Bible Society, which still sponsors the work of Bible translation and distribution around the world.

Elias Boudinot Jr.

PROTECTOR

"... as a guardian carries a nursing child ..."

NUMBERS 11:12

ETERNAL VIGILANCE

In his Farewell Address in 1837, President Andrew Jackson stated:

> *But you must remember, my fellow citizens, that eternal vigilance by the people is the price of liberty, and that you must pay the price if you wish to secure the blessing.*
>
> *You have no longer any cause to fear danger from abroad; your strength and power are well known throughout the civilized world, as well as the high and gallant bearing of your sons. It is from within, among yourselves—from cupidity, from corruption, from disappointed ambition and inordinate thirst for power—that factions will be formed and liberty endangered. It is against such designs, whatever disguise the actors may assume, that you have especially to guard yourselves. You have the highest of human trusts committed to your care. Providence has showered on this favored land blessings without number, and has chosen you as the guardians of freedom, to preserve it for the benefit of the human race. May He who holds in His hands the destinies of nations make you worthy of the favors He has bestowed and enable you, with pure hearts and pure hands and sleepless vigilance, to guard and defend to the end of time the great charge He has committed to your keeping.*

Andrew Jackson

THE FIRST BOOK PUBLISHED IN THE AMERICAN COLONIES

When the Pilgrim Fathers arrived at Plymouth, Massachusetts, the influence of the Bible and their Christian faith over their lives and literature came with them. A mere 20 years later, *The Bay Psalm Book* (originally titled *The Whole Booke of Psalmes Faithfully Translated into English Metre*) was printed in 1640 in Cambridge, Massachusetts. It was the first book printed in the colonies as well as the first book entirely written in the colonies. The first printing press in New England was purchased and imported specifically to print this volume.

The early residents of the Massachusetts Bay Colony brought with them several books of Psalms in metrical translations into English, but they were dissatisfied with the translations from Hebrew and hired "thirty pious and learned Ministers" to undertake a new translation. It represented a sacred value held by the Puritans—a faithful translation of God's Word, to be sung in worship by the entire congregation. Given the harsh living condition of those early years, it was a remarkable achievement.

The Bay Psalm Book went through several editions and remained in use for well over a century. This psalter and *The New England Primer* were, next to the Bible, the most commonly owned books in seventeenth-century New England.

The Bay Psalm Book

MORAL STRENGTH

"If a man ... swears an oath to bind himself by some agreement, he shall not break his word ..."

NUMBERS 30:2

RELIGION AND MORALITY

In his Farewell Address in 1796, President George Washington put his finger on the importance of preserving a freedom of religion within a society:

Of all the dispositions and habits which lead to political prosperity, religion and morality are indispensable supports. In vain would that man claim the tribute of patriotism who should labor to subvert these great pillars of human happiness—these firmest props of the duties of men and citizens. The mere politician, equally with the pious man, ought to respect and to cherish them. A volume could not trace all their connections with private and public felicity. Let it simply be asked, "Where is the security for property, for reputation, for life, if the sense of religious obligation desert the oaths which are the instruments of investigation in courts of justice?" And let us with caution indulge the supposition that morality can be maintained without religion. Whatever may be conceded to the influence of refined education on minds of peculiar structure, reason and experience both forbid us to expect that national morality can prevail in exclusion of religious principle.

It is substantially true that virtue or morality is a necessary spring of popular government. The rule indeed extends with more or less force to every species of free government. Who that is a sincere friend to it can look with indifference upon attempts to shake the foundation of the fabric?

George Washington

THE BIBLE OF THE REVOLUTION

Until the American Revolution, America's Bibles had been shipped in from England. When that supply was cut off and supplies dwindled in 1777, Congress resolved to import 20,000 copies of the Bible from other countries, based on a Congressional committee's determination that "the use of the Bible is so universal and its importance so great."

That resolution was not acted upon, though, and the need remained. Robert Aitken of Philadelphia published a New Testament in 1777 and followed it with three additional editions. In early 1781, he petitioned Congress and received the approval to print the entire Bible. Thus originated the first American printing of the English Bible in 1782, what has come to be called the "Bible of the Revolution."

W. P. Strickland, an early American historian, said of this Bible publication: "Who, in view of this fact, will call in question the assertion that this is a Bible nation? Who will charge the government with indifference to religion when the first Congress of the States assumed all the rights and performed all the duties of a Bible society long before such an institution had an existence in the world?"

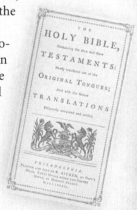

Aitken Bible 1782

29

INSPIRING

SAMUEL MORSE

"... Oh, what God has done!"

NUMBERS 23:23

Samuel Morse (1791–1872), an accomplished artist by profession, was captivated with the notion that electricity could be used to transmit messages instantly. He worked for years to become the creator of a single wire telegraph system, and co-inventor, with Alfred Vail, of the Morse Code, with letters represented by dots and dashes, to convey the telegraph message. His invention in the 1830s revolutionized and changed forever the realm of communications.

Although Morse had a patent, it took him years of failures and poverty before he was able to secure financial backing to implement his project. About those years, he said, "The only gleam of hope ... is from confidence in God. When I look upward it calms any apprehension for the future, and I seem to hear a voice saying: 'If I clothe the lilies of the field, shall I not also clothe you?' Here is my strong confidence, and I will wait patiently for the direction of Providence."

In 1843, Congress finally awarded Morris $30,000 to construct a telegraphic line between Baltimore and Washington. By Friday May 24, 1844, the lines were ready, and the words of the first official message were sent: "What hath God wrought!" selected from Numbers 23:23, in recognition that it was God who had inspired and sustained Morse throughout.

Samuel Morse

"WITHOUT GOD"

In August 1984, Ronald Reagan spoke to an ecumenical prayer breakfast in Dallas, Texas, and stated:

We establish no religion in this country, nor will we ever. We command no worship. We mandate no belief. But we poison our society when we remove its theological underpinnings. We court corruption when we leave it bereft of belief. All are free to believe or not believe; all are free to practice a faith or not. But those who believe must be free to speak of and act on their belief, to apply moral teaching to public questions.

I submit to you that the tolerant society is open to and encouraging of all religions. And this does not weaken us; it strengthens us. . . .

Without God, there is no virtue, because there's no prompting of the conscience. Without God, we're mired in the material, that flat world that tells us only what the senses perceive. Without God, there is a coarsening of the society. And without God, democracy will not and cannot long endure. If we ever forget that we're One Nation Under God, then we will be a nation gone under.

FAITH

. . . having no hope and without God in the world.

EPHESIANS 2:12

Ronald Reagan

31

COURAGE

. . . and they did not love their lives to the death.

REVELATION 12:11

"LET'S ROLL!"

On the morning of September 11, 2001, United Flight 93 from Newark to San Francisco was hijacked by terrorists who claimed to have a bomb. With telephone confirmation that other planes had hit the Twin Towers of the World Trade Center, the passengers understood the hijackers' intent.

Todd Beamer, a thirty-two-year-old businessman picked up a seat-back phone and reached Lisa Jefferson, a GTE supervisor. He told her that he and others were going to "jump on" a hijacker who was guarding the passengers in the rear. Beamer asked her to pray the Lord's Prayer with him. He also made her promise to call his wife, Lisa, and tell her that he loved her and their two little boys.

Dropping the phone after talking with Jefferson, Beamer said, "Jesus help me." Then after reciting Psalm 23, he said, "Are you guys ready? Okay, let's roll." Those were the unforgettable last words Beamer said before he and others rushed the hijackers of United Airlines Flight 93. There were screams, then silence.

Brave American civilians, complete strangers, rose against impossible odds and tried to save the 757-200 aircraft. In doing so, they made the ultimate patriotic sacrifice. United Flight 93 crashed into a large field near Shanksville, Pennsylvania, killing all forty-four aboard. Of the four hijacked planes that morning, United 93 was the only one that failed to hit a targeted site.

United Flight 93 Memorial

"I Am an American"

On June 2, 1995, U.S. Air Force Captain Scott O'Grady was patrolling the United Nations designated no-fly zone over war torn Bosnia when his F-16 fighter was struck by a surface-to-air missile at 27,000 feet above the Earth. He desperately pulled his ejection lever and was catapulted into the sky at 350 miles per hour. Remarkably, he managed to land unscathed in enemy territory.

He trusted in the LORD God of Israel . . .

2 KINGS 18:5

For six incredible days and nights, O'Grady eluded capture by the Bosnian Serbs who relentlessly hunted him. Utilizing his survival training to the maximum, O'Grady said it was also his faith in God that sustained him. On his third day on the ground, he experienced the love of God to such a level that it took away his fear of death. On the sixth day in a daring daylight rescue, an elite team of Marines moved in with a chopper, dodged enemy fire, and pulled the young American hero to safety.

At a national press conference following his triumphant return, O'Grady said, "If it wasn't for my love for God and God's love for me, I wouldn't be here right now." His inspirational and patriotic story is a brilliant testimony to Article 6 of the United States Military Code of Conduct: "I will never forget that I am an American, fighting for freedom, responsible for my actions, and dedicated to the principles which made my country free. I will trust in my God and in the United States of America."

Scott O'Grady

33

HOPE

...that you may prosper in all things...

3 John 2

STAYING TRUE TO THE CHRISTIAN RELIGION

Daniel Webster (1782–1852) was a leading American statesman and considered one of the greatest orators in American history. He served as a U.S. congressman, senator, and as the Secretary of State for three different presidents.

In a speech given before the Historical Society of New York, February 23, 1852, he said:

If we and our posterity shall be true to the Christian religion, if we and they shall live always in the fear of God, and shall respect His commandments, if we and they shall maintain just moral sentiments and such conscientious convictions of duty as shall control the heart and life, we may have the highest hopes of the future fortunes of our country; and if we maintain those institutions of government and that political union, exceeding all praise as much as it exceeds all former examples of political associations, we may be sure of one thing, that while our country furnishes material for a thousand masters of the historic art, it will afford no topic for a Gibbon. It will have no decline and fall. It will go on prospering and to prosper.

But if we and our posterity reject religious institutions and authority, violate the rules of eternal justice, trifle with the injunctions of morality, and recklessly destroy the political constitution which holds us together, no man can tell how sudden a catastrophe may overwhelm us that shall bury all our glory in profound obscurity.

Daniel Webster

34

How to Be Successful

> *"Do you still hold fast to your integrity?"*
>
> Job 2:9

William Bross (1813–1890) was a highly successful American journalist, the copublisher of the *Chicago Tribune*. In an interview, he discussed his success:

Q. What maxims have had a strong influence on your life and helped to your success?

A. *The Proverbs of Solomon and other Scriptures. They were quoted a thousand times by my honored father and caused an effort to do my duty each day, under a constant sense of obligation to my Savior and fellow man.*

Q. What do you consider essential elements of success for a young man entering upon such a profession as yours?

A. *Sterling, unflinching integrity in all matters, public and private. Let everyone do his whole duty, both to God and man. Let him follow earnestly the teachings of the Scriptures and eschew infidelity in all its forms.*

Q. What, in your observation, have been the chief causes of the numerous failures in the life of business and professional men?

A. *Want of integrity, careless of the truth, reckless in thought and expression, lack of trust in God, and a disregard of the teachings of His Holy Word, bad company, and bad morals in any of their many phases.*

William Bross

SELFLESS

*But the centurion ...
kept them from their
purpose ...*

ACTS 27:43

A POLICEMAN'S PRAYER

*When I start my tour of duty, God,
Wherever crime may be,
As I walk the darkened streets alone,
Let me be close to thee.*

*Please give me understanding
With both the young and old.
Let me listen with attention
Until their story's told.*

*Let me never make a judgment
In a rash or callous way,
But let me hold my patience ...
Let each man have his say.*

*Lord, if some dark and dreary night,
I must give my life,
Lord, with your everlasting love
protect my children and my wife.*

Author Unknown

A LEGACY OF SUCCESS

At age six, Henry John Heinz (1844–1919) started helping his mother tend a small garden behind the family home. At twelve, he was working three and one-half acres of garden, using a horse and cart for his three-times-a-week deliveries to grocery stores in Pittsburgh. He went on to found his own company and named it 57 Varieties. H. J. Heinz Company was incorporated in 1905, which today sells more than 1,300 products worldwide ranging from ketchup to baby food.

Henry Heinz was deeply involved in the promotion of the Sunday school in Pittsburgh and around the world. His company was noted for pioneering safe and sanitary food preparation and for being ahead of its time in employee relations, providing free medical benefits and swimming and gymnasium facilities. Women held positions of larger responsibilities in his business, including making them supervisors. Heinz earned his reputation for enhancing the working and living conditions of his workers.

In his will, Heinz said, "I desire to set forth at the very beginning of this will, as the most important item in it, a confession of my faith in Jesus Christ as my Savior. I also desire to bear witness to the fact that throughout my life, in which there were unusual joys and sorrows, I have been wonderfully sustained by my faith in God through Jesus Christ. This legacy was left me by my consecrated mother, a woman of strong faith, and to it I attribute any success I have attained."

Henry John Heinz

37

PRAYER

... and their prayer came up to His holy dwelling place, to heaven.

2 CHRONICLES 30:27

GOVERNMENT PAID LEGISLATIVE CHAPLAINS

Warren Earl Burger was Chief Justice of the U.S. Supreme Court from 1969 to 1986. He delivered the court's opinion in the 1982 case of *Marsh v. Chambers*, regarding chaplains opening legislative sessions with prayer:

The men who wrote the First Amendment religion clause did not view paid legislative chaplains and opening prayers as a violation of that amendment . . . the practice of opening sessions with prayer has continued without interruption ever since that early session of Congress.

It can hardly be thought that in the same week the members of the first Congress voted to appoint and pay a chaplain for each House and also voted to approve the draft of the First Amendment . . . (that) they intended to forbid what they had just declared acceptable.

[Prayer and chaplains] are deeply embedded in the history and tradition of this country.

The legislature by majority vote invites a clergyman to give a prayer, neither the inviting nor the giving nor the hearing of the prayer is making a law. On this basis alone . . . the sayings of prayers, per se, in the legislative halls at the opening session in not prohibited by the First and Fourteenth Amendments.

Warren Earl Burger

38

The "Holy Experiment"

William Penn (1644–1718), the founder of Pennsylvania, had been imprisoned in England more than three times for his faith as a Quaker. While imprisoned in the Tower of London for eight months, he wrote the classic book, *No Cross, No Crown,* in which he stated:

No pain, no palm; no thorns, no throne; no gall, no glory; no cross, no crown.

Charity

But concerning brotherly love . . . you yourselves are taught by God to love one another. . . .

1 Thessalonians 4:9

In 1682, Penn established the Pennsylvania colony as a land of religious freedom, granting toleration to every denomination. He printed advertisements in six different languages and sent them across Europe. Soon Quakers, Mennonites, Lutherans, Dunkards (Church of the Brethren), Amish, Moravians, Huguenots (French Protestants), Catholics, and Jews from England, Sweden, Wales, Germany, Scotland, Ireland, and Holland began arriving in his "holy experiment." To emphasize his plan for Christians working together, he planned and named their city "Philadelphia," which is Greek for "City of Brotherly Love." His concept was that religion is not to be limited to a Sunday ceremonial ritual, but should be an integral aspect of every day life, demonstrated by working with others.

William Penn

FAMILY VALUES

... husbands of one wife, ruling their children and their own houses well.

1 TIMOTHY 3:12

THE CORNERSTONE OF AMERICAN SOCIETY

Ronald Reagan, the 40th President of the United States (1981–1989), wrote:

The family has always been the cornerstone of American society. Our families nurture, preserve, and pass on to each succeeding generation the values we share and cherish, values that are the foundation for our freedoms. In the family, we learn our first lessons of God and man, love and discipline, rights and responsibilities, human dignity and human frailty.

Our families give us daily examples of these lessons being put into practice. In raising and instructing our children, in providing personal and compassionate care for the elderly, in maintaining the spiritual strength of religious commitment among our people—in these and other ways, America's families make immeasurable contributions to America's well-being.

Today more than ever, it is essential that these contributions not be taken for granted and that each of us remember that the strength of our families is vital to the strength of our nation.

Ronald and Nancy Reagan and family

Boston Tea Party

The Lord has made bare His holy arm . . .

Isaiah 52:10

The Stamp Act of 1765 and the Townshend Acts of 1767 had angered American colonists regarding British decisions on imposing intolerable taxes on the colonies without representation in the Westminster Parliament. In March 1770, the crisis culminated in the deaths of five American colonists killed by British soldiers who were commandeering homes. Early in 1773, the men of Marlborough, Massachusetts, declared unanimously:

Death is more eligible than slavery. A free-born people are not required by the religion of Jesus Christ to submit to tyranny, but may make use of such power as God has given them to recover and support their laws and liberties. . . . [We] implore the Ruler above the skies, that He would make bare His arm in defense of His Church and people, and let Israel go.

On December 16, 1773, the Sons of Liberty, a band of Boston patriots, threw the cargo of 342 chests of tea from a British East India Company ship into the Boston Harbor. The British government responded by closing the port of Boston, enacting other laws that were known as the "Intolerable Acts," and charging John Hancock, Samuel Adams, Joseph Warren, and Benjamin Church with the "Crime of High Treason." At the very least, the Boston Tea Party rallied the support for revolutionaries in the thirteen colonies and sparked the Revolution.

The Boston Tea Party

41

WORSHIP

GOOD WORKS

"... a tree is known by its fruit."

MATTHEW 12:33

Benjamin Franklin, one of America's renowned Founding Fathers, wrote:

I can only show my gratitude for these mercies from God, by a readiness to help His other children and my brethren. For I do not think that thanks and compliments, though repeated weekly, can discharge our real obligations to each other, and much less those to our Creator.

You will see in this my notion of good works, that I am far from expecting to merit heaven by them. By heaven we understand a state of happiness, infinite in degree, and eternal in duration. I can do nothing to deserve such rewards. . . .

The faith you mention has certainly its use in the world. I do not desire to see it diminished, nor would I endeavor to lessen it in any man. But I wish it were more productive of good works than I have generally seen it; I mean real good works; works of kindness, charity, mercy, and public spirit; not holiday keeping, sermon reading or hearing; performing church ceremonies, or making long prayers, filled with flatteries and compliments. . . .

The worship of God is a duty; the hearing and reading of sermons may be useful; but, if men rest in hearing and praying, as too many do, it is as if a tree should value itself on being watered and putting forth leaves, though it never produce any fruit.

Benjamin Franklin

George Washington's "Earnest Prayer"

The prayer below was written by Washington at Newburgh, New York, at the close of the Revolutionary War on June 14, 1783. It was sent to the thirteen governors of the newly freed states in a "Circular Letter Addressed to the Governors of all the States on the Disbanding of the Army."

PRAYER

Elijah was a man with a nature like ours, and he prayed earnestly ...

JAMES 5:17

I now make it my earnest prayer that God would have you, and the State over which you preside, in His holy protection; that He would incline the hearts of the citizens to cultivate a spirit of subordination and obedience to government, to entertain a brotherly affection and love for one another, for their fellow-citizens of the United States at large, and particularly for brethren who have served in the field; and finally that He would most graciously be pleased to dispose us all to do justice, to love mercy, and to demean ourselves with that charity, humility, and pacific temper of mind, which were the characteristics of the Divine Author of our blessed religion, and without an humble imitation of whose example in these things, we can never hope to be a happy nation.

George Washington

EQUIPPER

ON CIVIL LIBERTY

"'You shall love . . . your neighbor as yourself.'"

LUKE 10:27

Noah Webster (1758–1843) was an American lexicographer, textbook author, spelling reformer, political writer, word enthusiast, and editor. He has been called the "Father of American Scholarship and Education." In his public school textbook *History of the United States,* published in 1832, he stated:

Almost all the civil liberty now enjoyed in the world owes its origin to the principles of the Christian religion.

It is the sincere desire of the writer that our citizens should early understand that the genuine source of correct republican principles is the Bible, particularly the New Testament or the Christian religion.

The religion which has introduced civil liberty is the religion of Christ and His apostles, which enjoins humility, piety, and benevolence; which acknowledges in every person a brother, or a sister, and a citizen with equal rights. This is genuine Christianity, and to this we owe our free constitutions of government.

The moral principles and precepts contained in the Scriptures ought to form the basis of all of our civil constitutions and laws. . . . All the miseries and evils which men suffer from vice, crime, ambition, injustice, oppression, slavery, and war, proceed from their despising or neglecting the precepts contained in the Bible.

Noah Webster

Duty—Honor—Country

In his farewell speech to Corps of Cadets at West Point, General Douglas MacArthur gave a moving tribute to the ideals that inspire the great American soldier. For as long as other Americans serve their country courageously and honorably, his words will live on. The following excerpt from May 1962 is one small paragraph of his famous speech:

Duty—Honor—Country.
   The code which those words perpetuate embraces the highest moral laws and will stand the test of any ethics or philosophies ever promulgated for the uplift of mankind. Its requirements are for the things that are right, and its restraints are from the things that are wrong. The soldier, above all other men, is required to practice the greatest act of religious training—sacrifice. In battle and in the face of danger and death, he discloses those divine attributes which his Maker gave when He created man in His own image. No physical courage and no brute instinct can take the place of the Divine help which alone can sustain him. However horrible the incidents of war may be, the soldier who is called upon to offer and to give his life for his country is the noblest development of mankind.

Douglas MacArthur

PROTECTOR

"Be strong and of good courage; do not be afraid ..."

JOSHUA 1:9

Captain Russell Rippetoe was a member of the Alpha Company, 3rd Battalion, 75th Ranger Regiment, serving in Operation Iraqi Freedom in March 2003. Previously, while serving in Afghanistan, Rippetoe saw men die for the first time; and it brought a renewal to his Christian faith and a new passion for the Bible, which he carried in his backpack. On the chain around his neck, he wore a "Shield of Strength," a 1-by-2-inch emblem that displays a U.S. flag on one side and the words from Joshua 1:9 on the other. In his combat diary dated March 27, Rippetoe had written: "Think about what Mom and I talked about: all things happening for a reason, and God knows the reason."

On April 3, 2003, Alpha Company was manning a nighttime checkpoint near the Hadithah Dam in western Iraq when a vehicle approached. Suddenly, a woman jumped out and cried, "I'm hungry. I need food and water!" Protecting his men, Rippetoe gave the order to "hold back" as he moved toward the woman to see how he could help. When she hesitated, the driver detonated a car bomb that killed Captain Rippetoe, Sergeant Nino Livaudais, and Specialist Ryan Long, and wounded others.

Rippetoe believed the ancient words given to Joshua: ". . . the Lord my God is with me wherever I go." That he died trying to help someone else came as no surprise to those who knew him. He became the first casualty of the Iraq conflict to be buried at Arlington National Cemetery, the hallowed ground that is memorial to more than 250,000 American soldiers spanning back to the Revolutionary War.

Arlington National Cemetary

THE NORTHWEST ORDINANCE

MORAL STRENGTH

"You shall teach them diligently to your children ..."

DEUTERONOMY 6:7

On July 13, 1787, the Continental Congress passed the "Northwest Ordinance," which declared that the United States intended to settle the region north of the Ohio River and east of the Mississippi River. It set up the method by which new states would be admitted to the Union, giving them the same rights and powers as the established states, including the freedom of religion. Interestingly, it also stated the importance that Congress attached to religion: "Religion, morality, and knowledge being necessary to good government and the happiness of mankind, schools and the means of education shall forever be encouraged."

While the exact meaning of this sentence is still hotly debated, it is certainly positive legislation regarding religion and morality. James Wilson, one of only six Founders to have signed both the Declaration of Independence and the Constitution, pronounced in his law lectures at the University of Pennsylvania: "Far from being rivals or enemies, religion and law are twin sisters, friends, and mutual assistants." Not surprisingly, throughout American history up until the middle years of the twentieth century, government looked positively on both religion and morality. Various states worked out particular arrangements reflecting their particular circumstances, but in each case, religious freedom was respected while religion was looked upon as part of the common good, a "seedbed of virtue" contributing to American society.

James Wilson

47

INSPIRING

"... to give you a future and a hope."

JEREMIAH 29:11

"THE AMERICAN SOUND"

Few presidents had the ability to ignite hope in the hearts of those who love liberty more than President Ronald Reagan. In his Second Inaugural Address in 1985, he stated:

> *History is a ribbon, always unfurling; history is a journey. And as we continue our journey, we think of those who traveled before us. ... Now we hear again the echoes of our past: a general falls to his knees in the hard snow of Valley Forge; a lonely president paces the darkened halls and ponders his struggle to preserve the Union; the men of the Alamo call out encouragement to each other; a settler pushes west and sings a song, and the song echoes out forever and fills the unknowing air.*
>
> *It is the American sound. It is hopeful, big-hearted, idealistic, daring, decent, and fair. That's our heritage; that is our song. We sing it still. For all our problems, our differences, we are together as of old, as we raise our voices to the God who is the Author of this most tender music. And may He continue to hold us close as we fill the world with our sound—sound in unity, affection, and love—one people under God, dedicated to the dream of freedom that He has placed in the human heart, called upon now to pass that dream on to a waiting and hopeful world.*

Ronald Reagan

THE FOUNDATION OF AMERICA

DEFENDER

... united together as one man.

JUDGES 20:11

On September 11, 2001, in his address to the American people, President George Bush stated:

The pictures of airplanes flying into buildings, fires burning, huge structures collapsing, have filled us with disbelief, terrible sadness, and a quiet, unyielding anger. These acts of mass murder were intended to frighten our nation into chaos and retreat. But they have failed; our country is strong.

A great people has been moved to defend a great nation. Terrorist attacks can shake the foundations of our biggest buildings, but they cannot touch the foundation of America. These acts shattered steel, but they cannot dent the steel of American resolve.

America was targeted for attack because we're the brightest beacon for freedom and opportunity in the world. And no one will keep that light from shining.

Today, our nation saw evil, the very worst of human nature. And we responded with the best of America—with the daring of our rescue workers, with the caring for strangers and neighbors who came to give blood and help in any way they could.

This is a day when all Americans from every walk of life unite in our resolve for justice and peace. America has stood down enemies before, and we will do so this time. None of us will ever forget this day. Yet, we go forward to defend freedom and all that is good and just in our world.

George W. Bush

49

SERVICE

"... whoever desires to become great among you shall be your servant."

MARK 10:43

THE USE OF POWER

In his 1989 Inaugural Address, George H.W. Bush stated:

We meet on democracy's front porch, a good place to talk as neighbors and as friends. For this is a day when our nation is made whole, when our differences, for a moment, are suspended.

And my first act as President is a prayer. I ask you to bow your heads:

Heavenly Father, we bow our heads and thank You for Your love. Accept our thanks for the peace that yields this day and the shared faith that makes its continuance likely. Make us strong to do Your work, willing to heed and hear Your will, and write on our hearts these words: "Use power to help people." For we are given power not to advance our own purposes, nor to make a great show in the world, nor a name. There is but one just use of power, and it is to serve people. Help us to remember it, Lord. Amen.

George H.W. Bush

LIFE AND IMMORTALITY

John McLean (1785–1861), a U.S. Postmaster General and Justice of the U.S. Supreme Court, wrote:

> No one can estimate or describe the salutary influence of the Bible. What would the world be without it? Compare the dark places of the earth, where the light of the Gospel has not penetrated, with those where it has been proclaimed and embraced in all its purity. Life and immortality are brought to light by the Scriptures.
>
> Aside from Revelation, darkness rests upon the world and upon the future. There is no ray of light to shine upon our pathway; there is no star of hope. We begin our speculations as to our destiny in conjecture, and they end in uncertainty. We know not that there is a God, a heaven, or a hell, or any day of general account, when the wicked and the righteous shall be judged.
>
> The Bible has shed a glorious light upon the world. It shows us that in the coming day we must answer for the deeds done in the body. It has opened us to a new and living way, so plainly marked out that no one can mistake it. The price paid for our redemption shows the value of our immortal souls.

HOPE

... shone in our hearts to give the light ...

2 CORINTHIANS 4:6

John McLean

COURAGE

"The LORD is with you, you mighty man of valor!"

JUDGES 6:12

FRANCIS MARION, THE "SWAMP FOX"

Francis Marion (1732–1795) was a brigadier general in the South Carolina Militia during the American Revolutionary War. He became known as the "Swamp Fox" because he set up his base of operations in a swamp. "Marion's Brigade" was a volunteer force that could assemble at a moment's notice, hit British and Loyalist units and garrisons, and then disappear into the swamps. He is considered one of the fathers of modern guerrilla warfare.

While the British occupied most of the southern colonies, large-scale resistance was impossible. Marion and his patriot unit was a powerful force in the south, as Nathanael Greene later wrote in praise: "Surrounded on every side with a superior force, hunted from every quarter with veteran troops, you have found means to elude their attempts and keep alive the expiring hopes of an oppressed militia."

After the war, Marion served in the state Senate of South Carolina for several terms. He stated: "Who can doubt that God created us to be happy, and thereto made us to love one another? It is plainly written as the Gospel. The heart is sometimes so embittered that nothing but Divine love can sweeten it, so enraged that devotion can only becalm it, and so broken down that it takes all the forces of heavenly hope to raise it. In short, the religion of Jesus Christ is the only sure and controlling power over sin."

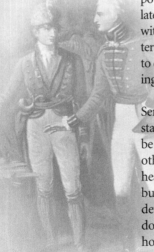

Francis Marion, left, and a British officer

52

THE FOURTH OF JULY CELEBRATION

. . . that without fail they should celebrate these two days every year . . .

ESTHER 9:27

On July 3, 1776, following the signing of the Declaration of Independence, John Adams wrote to his wife, reflecting on what he had shared in Congress concerning the importance of that day:

The second day of July 1776 will be the most memorable epoch in the history of America. I am apt to believe that it will be celebrated by succeeding generations as the great anniversary festival. It ought to be commemorated as the day of deliverance, by solemn acts of devotion to God Almighty. It ought to be solemnized with pomp and parade, with shows, games, sports, guns, bells, bonfires, and illuminations, from one end of this continent to the other, from this time forward forever.

You will think me transported with enthusiasm, but I am not. I am well aware of the toil and blood and treasure that it will cost to maintain this Declaration and support and defend these States. Yet through all the gloom I can see the rays of ravishing light and glory. I can see that the end is worth more than all the means; that posterity will triumph in that day's transaction, even though we [may regret] it, which I trust in God we shall not.

53

TRUTH

And if Christ is not risen, your faith is futile ...

1 Corinthians 15:17

True History or Consummate Fraud?

Daniel Webster (1782–1852), a leading American statesman during the nation's Antebellum Period, declared:

The Gospel is either true history, or it is a consummate fraud; it is either a reality or an imposition. Christ was what He professed to be, or He was an imposter. There is no other alternative.

His spotless life in His earnest enforcement of the truth—His suffering in its defense, forbid us to suppose that He was suffering an illusion of a heated brain. Every act of His pure and holy life shows that He was the author of truth, the advocate of truth, the earnest defender of truth, and the uncompromising sufferer for truth.

Now, considering the purity of His doctrines, the simplicity of His life, and the sublimity of His death, is it possible that He would have died for an illusion? In all His preaching the Savior made no popular appeals; His discourses were always directed to the individual. Christ and His apostles sought to impress upon every man the conviction that he must stand or fall alone—he must live for himself, and die for himself, and give up his account to the omniscient God as though he were the only dependent creature in the universe. The Gospel leaves the individual sinner alone with himself and his God.

Daniel Webster

THE FIRST NATIONAL DAY OF THANKSGIVING

... in wrath remember mercy.

HABAKKUK 3:2

In the midst of the Civil War, President Abraham Lincoln initiated the first annual National Day of Thanksgiving and Praise on October 3, 1863, issuing a formal Proclamation, passed by an Act of Congress:

... No human counsel hath devised nor hath any mortal hand worked out these great things. They are the gracious gifts of the Most High God, who, while dealing with us in anger for our sins, hath nevertheless remembered mercy. It has seemed to me fit and proper that they should be solemnly, reverently, and gratefully acknowledged as with one heart and one voice by the whole American People. I do therefore invite my fellow citizens in every part of the United States, and also those who are at sea and those who are sojourning in foreign lands, to set apart and observe the last Thursday of November next, as a day of Thanksgiving and Praise to our beneficent Father who dwelleth in the Heavens.

And I recommend to them that while offering up the ascriptions justly due to Him for such singular deliverances and blessings, they do also, with humble penitence for our national perverseness and disobedience, commend to His tender care all those who have become widows, orphans, mourners, or sufferers in the lamentable civil strife in which we are unavoidably engaged, and fervently implore the interposition of the Almighty Hand to heal the wounds of the nation and to restore it as soon as may be consistent with the Divine purposes to the full enjoyment of peace, harmony, tranquility, and Union.

Abraham Lincoln

55

FAITH

THE DESIGNER OF THE UNIVERSE

Wernher von Braun (1912–1977), the director of NASA and known as "The Father of the American Space Program," stated in a published article in May 1974:

> One cannot be exposed to the law and order of the universe without concluding that there must be design and purpose behind it all. . . . The better we understand the intricacies of the universe and all it harbors, the more reason we have found to marvel at the inherent design upon which it is based. . . .

> To be forced to believe only one conclusion—that everything in the universe happened by chance—would violate the very objectivity of science itself. . . . What random process could produce the brains of a man or the system of the human eye? . . .

> They [evolutionists] challenge science to prove the existence of God. But must we really light a candle to see the sun? . . . They say they cannot visualize a Designer. Well, can a physicist visualize an electron? . . . What strange rationale makes some physicists accept the inconceivable electron as real while refusing to accept the reality of a Designer on the ground that they cannot conceive Him?

Wernher von Braun

56

Man as God's Coworker

SERVICE

George Washington Carver (1864–1943), an agricultural chemist who discovered three hundred uses for peanuts and hundreds more uses for soybeans, pecans, and sweet potatoes, shared some of his observations about God:

> *"... in Him we live and move and have our being ..."*
>
> ACTS 17:28

As a very small boy exploring the almost virgin woods of the old Carver place, I had the impression someone had just been there ahead of me. Things were so orderly, so clean, so harmoniously beautiful. A few years later in this same woods, I was to understand the meaning of this boyish impression ... because I was practically overwhelmed with the sense of some Great Presence. Not only had someone been there. Someone was there. ...

Years later when I read in the Scriptures, "In Him we live and move and have our being," I knew what the writer meant. Never since have I been without this consciousness of the Creator speaking to me. ... The out-of-doors has been to me more and more a great cathedral in which God could be continuously spoken to and heard from. ...

Man, who needed a purpose, a mission, to keep him alive, had one. He could be ... God's coworker. ... My purpose alone must be God's purpose—to increase the welfare and happiness of His people. ... Why, then, should we who believe in Christ be so surprised at what God can do with a willing man in a laboratory?

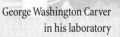

George Washington Carver in his laboratory

But the men of Judah ... remained loyal to their king.

2 SAMUEL 20:2

Noah Webster's *An American Dictionary of the English Language,* 1828

patriotism, n. Love of one's country; the passion which aims to serve one's country, either in defending it from invasion, or protecting its rights and maintaining its laws and institutions in vigor and purity. Patriotism is the characteristic of a good citizen, the noblest passion that animates a man in the character of a citizen.

Merriam-Webster's Collegiate Dictionary, Eleventh Edition, copyright © 2004

patriotism, n. Love for or devotion to one's country.

Note how the definitions have changed. Noah Webster's patriot defends his country with objective actions, versus the vague, subjective patriotism of one who only feels and expresses love for his country. True patriotism is not just an emotional feeling; it is action.

Webster's original definition includes a love for country, service to country, defense of country, protection of the rights of country, maintenance of the laws and institutions of country, preservation of religion and morality in public and private life, and puts the needs of the country above personal or partisan desires as well as above the favor of foreign nations.

THE GOVERNMENT AND NATIVITY SCENES

Warren Earl Burger, Chief Justice of the United States from 1969 to 1986, delivered the Supreme Court's opinion in the 1985 case of *Lynch v. Donnelly,* which upheld that the city of Pawtucket, Rhode Island, did not violate the Constitution by displaying a Nativity scene. Noting that presidential orders and proclamations from Congress have designated Christmas as a national holiday in religious terms for two centuries and in the Western world for twenty centuries, he wrote:

> *There is an unbroken history of official acknowledgment by all three branches of government of the role of religion in American life. . . . The Constitution does not require a complete separation of church and state. It affirmatively mandates accommodation, not merely tolerance, of all religions and forbids hostility towards any. . . . Anything less would require the "callous indifference" we have said was never intended by the Establishment Clause. Indeed, we have observed, such hostility would bring us into a "war with our national tradition as embodied in the First Amendment's guaranty of the free exercise of religion."*

Warren Earl Burger

59

WORSHIP

And let the whole earth be filled with His glory.

Psalm 72:19

Fill the World with His Glory

To celebrate the victorious conclusion of the Revolutionary War, Governor John Hancock of Massachusetts issued a Proclamation for a Day of Thanksgiving on December 11, 1783:

> *Whereas . . . these United States are not only happily rescued from the danger and calamities to which they have been so long exposed, but their freedom, sovereignty, and independence ultimately acknowledged.*
>
> *And whereas . . . the interposition of Divine Providence in our favor hath been most abundantly and most graciously manifested, and the citizens of these United States have every reason for praise and gratitude to the God of their salvation.*
>
> *Impressed therefore with an exalted sense of the blessings by which we are surrounded, and of our entire dependence on that Almighty Being from whose goodness and bounty they are derived; I do by and with the Advice of the Council appoint Thursday the eleventh day of December next (the day recommended by the Congress to all the States) to be religiously observed as a day of Thanksgiving and Prayer, that all the people may then assemble to celebrate . . . that He hath been pleased to continue to us the Light of the blessed Gospel; . . . That we also offer up fervent supplications . . . to cause pure religion and virtue to flourish . . . and to fill the world with His glory.*

John Hancock

"GOD, GIVE US MEN"

Josiah Gilbert Holland (1819–1881), a poet and the founder and editor of the popular *Scribner's Monthly* (afterward the *Century Magazine*), penned these famous words:

God, give us men! A time like this demands
    Strong minds, great hearts, true faith and ready hands;
    Men whom the lust of office does not kill;
Men whom the spoils of office can not buy;
    Men who possess opinions and a will;
Men who have honor; men who will not lie;
Men who can stand before a demagogue
    And damn his treacherous flatteries without winking!
Tall men, sun-crowned, who live above the fog
    In public duty, and in private
        thinking;
For while the rabble, with their thumb-
    worn creeds,
Their large professions and their little
    deeds,
Mingle in selfish strife, lo! Freedom
    weeps,
Wrong rules the land and waiting
    Justice sleeps.

DEFENDER

Defending the Unborn

Henry Hyde served thirty-two years in the House of Representatives and was described as a passionate, eloquent champion and powerful defender of the unborn and of American freedom. On July 16, 1993, he stated:

"That all men are created equal and are endowed by their Creator"— human beings upon creation, not upon birth. That is where our human dignity comes from. It comes from the Creator. It is an endowment, not an achievement.

By membership in the human family, we are endowed by our Creator with "inalienable rights." They can't be voted away by a jury or a court.

"Among which are life"—the first inalienable right, the first endowment from the Creator. That is mainstream America, the predicate for our Constitution, our country's birth certificate. To respect the right to life as an endowment from the Creator. . . .

It is the unborn who are the least of God's creatures. We have been told that whatsoever we do for the least of these we do unto Jesus.

Henry Hyde

Correcting Abuses

In July 1832, President Andrew Jackson vetoed the Bank Renewal Bill, preventing the rechartering of the Bank of the United States. Believing the bank was unauthorized by the Constitution and concentrated too much economic power in the hands of a small moneyed elite, he stated:

In the full enjoyment of the gifts of Heaven and the fruits of superior industry, economy, and virtue, every man is equally entitled to protection by law; but when the laws undertake to add to these natural and just advantages artificial distinctions, to grant titles, gratuities, and exclusive privileges, to make the rich richer and the potent more powerful, the humble members of society—the farmers, mechanics, and laborers—... have a right to complain of the injustice of their Government.

There are no necessary evils in government. Its evils exist only in its abuses. If it would confine itself to equal protection, and, as Heaven does its rains, shower its favors alike on the high and the low, the rich and the poor, it would be an unqualified blessing. In the act before me there seems to be a wide and unnecessary departure from these just principles. ...

For relief and deliverance let us firmly rely on that kind Providence which I am sure watches with peculiar care over the destinies of our Republic, and on the intelligence and wisdom of our countrymen. Through His abundant goodness and their patriotic devotion our liberty and Union will be preserved.

PROTECTOR

Moreover I saw ... in the place of righteousness, iniquity was there.

Ecclesiastes 3:16

Andrew Jackson

HUMILITY

"Turn to Me with all your heart, with fasting, with weeping, and with mourning."

JOEL 2:12

DAYS OF FASTING

After the Boston Tea Party, the British navy retaliated by blockading the port of Boston. The colonies surrounding Massachusetts responded with sympathy and action. On May 24, 1773, the House of Burgesses in Virginia proposed and approved a Day of Fasting, Humiliation, and Prayer:

This House, being deeply impressed with apprehension of the great dangers to be derived to British America from the hostile invasion of the city of Boston in our Sister Colony of Massachusetts Bay, whose commerce and harbor are, on the first day of June next, to be stopped by an armed force, deem it highly necessary that the said first day of June be set apart, by the members of this House, as a Day of Fasting, Humiliation, and Prayer, devoutly to implore the Divine interposition, for averting the heavy calamity which threatens destruction to our civil rights and the evils of civil war; to give us one heart and mind firmly opposed, by all just and proper means, every injury to American rights; and that the minds of his Majesty and his Parliament, may be inspired from above with wisdom, moderation, and justice, to remove from the loyal people of America all cause of danger from a continued pursuit of measures pregnant with their ruin.

The Boston Tea Party

CHRISTIAN MEN OF SCIENCE

... the wind whirls about continually, and comes again on its circuit.

ECCLESIASTES 1:6

Matthew Maury (1806–1873), nicknamed the "Pathfinder of the Seas" for having charted the ocean and wind currents while serving in the U.S. Navy, was considered the "Father of Modern Oceanography and Naval Meteorology" and later the "Scientist of the Seas." He wrote:

I have always found in my scientific studies, that, when I could get the Bible to say anything on the subject, it afforded me a firm platform to stand upon and a round in the ladder by which I could safely ascend.

As our knowledge of nature and her laws has increased, so has our knowledge of many passages of the Bible improved.

The Bible called the earth "the round world," yet for ages it was ... heresy for Christian men to say that the world is round; and, finally, sailors circumnavigated the globe and proved the Bible to be right, and saved Christian men of science from the stake.

And as for the general system of circulation which I have been so long endeavoring to describe, the Bible tells it all in a single sentence: "The wind goeth toward the South ... and returneth again to his circuits."

Matthew Maury

65

HOPE

"But on Mount Zion there shall be deliverance ..."

OBADIAH 17

"SAIL ON, O SHIP OF STATE!"

Henry Wadsworth Longfellow (1807–1882) was by far the most widely known and best-loved American poet of his time. He achieved a level of national and international prominence possibly unequaled in the literary history of the United States. A fervent abolitionist, his poem "The Building of a Ship" was a pro-Union allegory that speaks of his fear that the slavery issue would destroy the Union. Upon hearing the poem recited, President Lincoln was said to have wept:

Thou, too, sail on, O Ship of State!
Sail on, O Union, strong and great!
Humanity with all its fears,
With all the hopes of future years,
Is hanging breathless on thy fate! . . .

Our hearts, our hopes, are all with thee,
Our hearts, our hopes, our prayers, our tears,
Our faith triumphant o'er our fears,
Are all with thee—are all with thee!

In early 1941, President Franklin Roosevelt sent a handwritten letter to English Prime Minister Churchill and included the first five lines of Longfellow's poem, stating the verse "applies to you people as it does to us." Churchill wrote back that he was "deeply moved" and cited the letter as a symbol of the growing partnership between England and the United States. "Give us the tools," he told the president, "and we will finish the job!"

Henry Wadsworth Longfellow

RULES OF MORAL ACTION

MORAL STRENGTH

. . . leaving us an example, that you should follow His steps . . .

1 Peter 2:21

Wesley Merritt, a Major General in the Union Army during the Civil War and the superintendent of the U.S. Military Academy at West Point (1882–1887), stated:

The principles of life as taught in the Bible, the inspired Word, and exemplified in the matchless life of Him "who spake as never man spake," are the rules of moral action which have resulted in civilizing the world.

The testimony of great men, like Gladstone and his fellow statesmen; like Havelock and his fellow soldiers, who have made the teachings of the Scriptures their rule of conduct in life, are wonderful helps to men of lesser note and smaller intellectual and moral powers. One example, even of the smallest of these, more than offsets the efforts of an hundred unbelievers in active opposition.

They are the worthy followers of the religion of the Bible, and in their daily lives interpret the inimitable example and Divine precepts of the Son of God, our Savior.

Major General Wesley Merritt

67

DEFENDER

THE LAND OF THE BIBLE

Benjamin Franklin Morris (1810–1867), the Congregational minister and historian who wrote *The Christian Life and Character of the Civil Institutions of the United States* in 1864, stated:

> These fundamental objects of the Constitution are in perfect harmony with the revealed objects of the Christian religion. Union, justice, peace, the general welfare, and the blessings of civil and religious liberty, are the objects of Christianity, and always secured under its practical and beneficent reign.
>
> The state must rest upon the basis of religion, and it must preserve this basis, or itself must fall. But the support which religion gives to the state will obviously cease the moment religion loses its hold upon the popular mind.

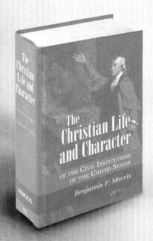

> This is a Christian nation, first in name, and secondly because of the many and mighty elements of a pure Christianity which have given it character and shaped its destiny from the beginning. It is preeminently the land of the Bible, of the Christian Church, and of the Christian Sabbath. . . . The chief security and glory of the United States of America has been, is now, and will be forever, the prevalence and domination of the Christian faith.

FACING FEAR IN DARK HOURS

In his First Inaugural Address, Franklin Delano Roosevelt, the 32nd President of the United States (1933–1945), proclaimed to the nation, as it just entered the Depression:

First of all, let me assert my firm belief that the only thing we have to fear is fear itself—nameless, unreasoning, unjustified terror which paralyzes needed efforts to convert retreat into advance. . . . In such a spirit on my part and on yours we face our common difficulties. They concern, thank God, only material things. . . .

Practices of the unscrupulous moneychangers stand indicted in the court of public opinion, rejected by the hearts and minds of men. . . . They know only the rules of a generation of self-seekers. They have no vision, and where there is no vision the people perish [Proverbs 29:18]. The moneychangers have fled from their high seats in the temple of our civilization. We may now restore that temple to the ancient truths. . . .

We face arduous days that lie before us in the warm courage of national unity; with the clear consciousness of seeking old and precious moral values. . . .

In this dedication of a nation we humbly ask the blessing of God. May He protect each and every one of us! May He guide me in the days to come.

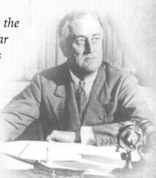

Franklin Delano Roosevelt

69

SELFLESS

"...from the burning fiery furnace..."

DANIEL 3:17

A FIREMAN'S PRAYER

When I am called to duty, God,
Wherever flame may rage,
Give me the strength to save some life,
Whatever be its age.

Help me embrace a little child
Before it is too late,
Or save an older person from
The horror of that fate.

Enable me to be alert
And hear the weakest shout,
And quickly and efficiently
To put the fire out.

I want to fill my calling and
To give the best in me,
To guard my every neighbor
And protect his property.

And if according to my fate,
I am to lose my life,
Please bless with Your protecting hand
My children and my wife.

Author Unknown

American Fireman,
Rushing to the Conflict
by Currier & Ives

"DUTY TO GOD"

The Boy Scouts of America believes that no member can grow into the best kind of citizen without recognizing an obligation to God. Accordingly, youth members and adult volunteer leaders obligate themselves to do their duty to God and be reverent as embodied in the Scout Oath and the Scout Law. But it hasn't been without its share of legal battles.

FREEDOM

"We have done what was our duty to do."

LUKE 17:10

In the 1993 case of *Welsh v. Boy Scouts of America*, the United States Court of Appeals—Seventh Circuit ruled that the Boy Scouts could keep the phrase "duty to God" in their oath, and as a private organization they had the right to exclude anyone who refused to take the oath. It stated:

The leadership of many in our government is a testimonial to the success of Boy Scout activities. . . . In recent years, single-parent families, gang activity, the availability of drugs, and other factors have increased the dire need for support structures like the Scouts.

When the government, in this instance, through the courts, seeks to regulate the membership of an organization like the Boy Scouts in a way that scuttles its founding principles, we run the risk of undermining one of the seedbeds of virtue that cultivate the sorts of citizens our nation so desperately needs.

Cases in 1995 and 1998 upheld the "duty to God" requirements for Scouts as well as leaders.

Boy Scouts of America 1941

WORSHIP

"Who can this be, that even the wind and the sea obey Him!"

MARK 4:41

"WHO BUT THE RULER OF THE WINDS?"

As the president of Yale College (1778–1795), Ezra Stiles gave a major Election Address entitled "The United States Elevated to Glory and Honor," before the governor and the General Assembly of Connecticut in May 1783, stating:

In our lowest and most dangerous state, in 1776 and 1777, we sustained ourselves against the British Army of sixty thousand troops, commanded by . . . the ablest generals Britain could procure throughout Europe, with a naval force of twenty-two thousand seamen in above eighty men-of-war.

Who but a Washington, inspired by Heaven, could have conceived the surprise move upon the enemy at Princeton—that Christmas eve when Washington and his army crossed the Delaware?

Who but the Ruler of the winds could have delayed the British reinforcements by three months of contrary ocean winds at a critical point of the war?

Or what but "a providential miracle" at the last minute detected the treacherous scheme of traitor Benedict Arnold, which would have delivered the American army, including George Washington himself, into the hands of the enemy?

On the French role in the Revolution, it is God who so ordered the balancing interests of nations as to produce an irresistible motive in the European maritime powers to take our part. . . .

The United States are under peculiar obligations to become a holy people unto the Lord our God.

Ezra Stiles

72

THE LAST BASTION OF FREEDOM

Richard Wurmbrand (1909–2001), a Romanian evangelical Christian minister and author who spent a total of fourteen years imprisoned in Romania for his faith, was also the founder of the Voice of the Martyrs, an interdenominational organization working with and for persecuted Christians around the world. In 1967, he expressed this view of America:

Every freedom-loving man has two fatherlands; his own and America. Today, America is the hope of every enslaved man, because it is the last bastion of freedom in the world. Only America has the power and spiritual resources to stand as a barrier between militant communism and the people of the world.

It is the last "dike" holding back the rampaging floodwaters of militant communism. If it crumples, there is no other dike, no other dam; no other line of defense to fall back upon.

America is the last hope of millions of enslaved peoples. They look to it as their second fatherland. In it lies their hopes and prayers.

I have seen fellow-prisoners in communist prisons beaten, tortured, with 50 pounds of chains on their legs—praying for America. . . . that the dike will not crumple; that it will remain free.

HOPE

"Where then is my hope?"

JOB 17:15

DEFENDER

For You formed my inward parts; You covered me in my mother's womb.

PSALM 139:13

IN DEFENSE OF LIFE

Pope John Paul II addressed a crowd of over 375,000 people from 70 different countries in a Mass celebrated at Cherry Creek State Park, Colorado, as a part of "World Youth Day" on August 15, 1993. He stated:

A "culture of death" seeks to impose itself on our desire to live, and live to the full. . . . In our own century, as at no other time in history, the "culture of death" has assumed a social and institutional form of legality to justify the most horrible crimes against humanity: genocide, "final solutions," "ethnic cleansings," and massive taking of lives of human beings even before they are born, or before they reach the natural point of death. . . .

In much of contemporary thinking, any reference to a "law" guaranteed by the Creator is absent. There remains only each individual's choice of this or that objective as convenient or useful in a given set of circumstances. No longer is anything considered intrinsically "good" and "universally binding."

The family especially is under attack. And the sacred character of Human Life is denied. Naturally, the weakest members of society are the most at risk. The unborn, children, the sick, the handicapped, the old, the poor and unemployed, the immigrant and refugee. . . .

You must feel the full urgency of the task. Woe to you if you do not succeed in defending life. The church needs your energies, your enthusiasm, your youthful ideas, in order to make the Gospel of Life penetrate the fabric of society, transforming people's hearts and the structures of society in order to create a civilization of true justice and love.

Pope John Paul II

THE BIBLE'S INFLUENCE ON THE FOUNDING FATHERS

In 1984, political scientists Donald Lutz and Charles Hyneman at the University of Houston wrote a paper regarding the research they had done to determine the sources that most influenced the development of American political thought during our nation's founding period. Over the course of ten years, they analyzed some 15,000 items of American political commentary published between 1760 and 1805, the Founding Era. This research paper, "The Relative Influence of European Writers on Late Eighteenth-Century American Political Thought," was published in *The American Political Science Review,* 78 (1984).

The researchers isolated 3,154 direct quotes made by the Founders over this period of time and identified the source of those quotes. The researchers discovered that 34 percent of the Founders' quotes came directly out of the Bible. Baron Charles de Montesquieu, a French legal philosopher, was quoted 8.3 percent of the time. Sir William Blackstone, a renowned English jurist whose *Commentaries on the Laws of England* were highly accepted in America, was next at 7.9 percent of the Founders' quotes, and John Locke, an English philosopher, was fourth with 2.9 percent.

While it is true that three-fourths of the biblical citations in the 1760 to 1805 sample came from reprinted sermons (one of the most popular types of political writing during these years), and only 9 percent of all citations came from secular literature, it is a reflection of the powerful role of the Bible upon the thinking of the Founding Fathers.

MORAL STRENGTH

"For who has despised the day of small things?"

ZECHARIAH 4:10

TRUE CHRISTIAN, TRUE CITIZEN

Theodore Roosevelt, the 26th President of the United States (1901–1909), the youngest man to hold the office, stated:

The true Christian is the true citizen, lofty of purpose, resolute in endeavor, ready for a hero's deeds, but never looking down on his task because it is cast in the day of small things; scornful of baseness, awake to his own duties as well as to his rights, following the higher law with reverence, and in this world doing all that in his power lies, so that when death comes he may feel that mankind is in some degree better because he lived.

Every thinking man, when he thinks, realizes that the teachings of the Bible are so interwoven and entwined with our whole civic and social life that it would be literally impossible for us to figure ourselves what that life would be if these standards were removed. We would lose almost all the standards by which we now judge both public and private morals; all the standards toward which we, with more or less resolution, strive to raise ourselves.

Theodore Roosevelt

76

YES, THERE IS HOPE

On September 14, 2001, in the aftermath of the September 11 attacks, Dr. Billy Graham led a national prayer and remembrance service at Washington National Cathedral in which he reminded every American:

This event reminds us of the brevity and the uncertainty of life. We never know when we too will be called into eternity. I doubt if even one of those people who got on those planes or walked into the World Trade Center or the Pentagon last Tuesday morning thought it would be the last day of their lives. It didn't occur to them. And that's why each of us needs to face our own spiritual need and commit ourselves to God and His will now.

Here in this majestic National Cathedral we see all around us symbols of the Cross. For the Christian, I'm speaking for the Christian now, the Cross tells us that God understands our sin and our suffering, for He took upon Himself in the person of Jesus Christ our sins and our suffering. And from the Cross, God declares, "I love you. I know the heartaches and the sorrows and the pains that you feel. But I love you."

The story does not end with the Cross, for Easter points us beyond the tragedy of the Cross to the empty tomb. It tells us that there is hope for eternal life, for Christ has conquered evil and death, and hell. Yes, there is hope.

Dr. Billy Graham

77

TRUTH

CHRISTIANITY AND COMMON LAW

At the age of thirty-two, Joseph Story became the youngest Associate Justice of the Supreme Court and served from 1811 to 1845, writing 286 opinions. He was also the Dane Professor of Law at Harvard and wrote many legal texts now considered classics. His three-volume set of *Commentaries on the Constitution of the United States* is still the standard treatise on the subject.

At a point in his life where Story doubted the truth of Christianity, he "labored and read with assiduous attention all of the arguments of its proof" and became committed to the principles of Christianity, which he repeatedly expressed throughout his lengthy legal career. It was his conviction that American law and legal practices must never be separated from Christian principles. As he explained:

> *One of the beautiful boasts of our municipal jurisprudence is that Christianity is a part of the Common Law. . . . There never has been a period in which the Common Law did not recognize Christianity as lying at its foundations. . . . [The law] pronounces illegal every contract offensive to [Christianity's] morals. It recognizes with profound humility [Christianity's] holidays and festivals, and obeys them [even to the point of suspending all government functions on those days]. It still attaches to persons believing in [Christianity's] divine authority the highest degree of competency as witnesses.*

Joseph Story

PURPOSE OF A PUBLIC EDUCATION

"... to serve the LORD your God with all your heart ..."

DEUTERONOMY 10:12

William Samuel Johnson (1727–1819), president of Columbia University (formerly King's College), said to the first graduating class after the Revolutionary War:

You have ... received a public education, the purpose whereof hath been to qualify you the better to serve your Creator and your country. ... Your first great duties ... are those you owe to Heaven, to your Creator and Redeemer. Let these be ever present to your minds and exemplified in your lives and conduct.

Imprint deep upon your minds the principles of piety toward God, and a reverence and fear of His holy name. The fear of God is the beginning of wisdom, and its consummation is everlasting felicity. ... Remember, too, that you are the redeemed of the Lord, that you are bought with a price, even the inestimable price of the precious blood of the Son of God. Adore Jehovah, therefore, as your God and your Judge. Love, fear, and serve Him as your Creator, Redeemer, and Sanctifier. Acquaint yourselves with Him in His Word and holy ordinances.

Make Him your friend and protector and your felicity is secured both here and hereafter. And with respect to particular duties to Him, it is your happiness that you are well assured that he best serves his Maker, who does most good to his country and to mankind.

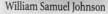

William Samuel Johnson

79

PROTECTOR

"He has shown you, O man, what is good . . ."

MICAH 6:8

A WISE AND FRUGAL GOVERNMENT

In his 1801 Inaugural Address, President Thomas Jefferson stated:

Sometimes it is said that man cannot be trusted with the government of himself. Can he, then, be trusted with the government of others? Or have we found angels in the forms of kings to govern him? Let history answer this question. Let us, then, with courage and confidence pursue our own federal and republican principles. . . .

Enlightened by a benign religion, professed, indeed, and practiced in various forms, yet all of them inculcating honesty, truth, temperance, gratitude, and the love of man; acknowledging and adoring an overruling Providence, which by all its dispensations proves that it delights in the happiness of man here and his greater happiness hereafter. With all these blessings, what more is necessary to make us a happy and prosperous people? Still one thing more, fellow citizens— a wise and frugal government, which shall restrain men from injuring one another, shall leave them otherwise free to regulate their own pursuits of industry and improvement, and shall not take from the mouth of labor the bread it has earned. . . .

You should understand what I deem the essential principles of our government. . . . Equal and exact justice to all men, of whatever state or persuasion, religious or political . . . the arraignment of all abuses at the bar of the public reason; freedom of religion; freedom of the press, and freedom of person under the protection of the habeas corpus and trial by jury impartially selected. . . .

Thomas Jefferson

80

RENDER HONOR TO THE CREATOR

James Madison, the fourth president of the United States and "Chief Architect of the Constitution," wrote:

Remember now your Creator in the days of your youth . . .

ECCLESIASTES 12:1

The religion then of every man must be left to the conviction and conscience of every man; and it is the right of every man to exercise it as these may dictate. This right is in its nature an unalienable right. It is unalienable, because the opinions of men, depending only on the evidence contemplated by their own minds cannot follow the dictates of other men: It is unalienable also, because what is here a right toward men, is a duty toward the Creator. It is the duty of every man to render to the Creator such homage and such only as he believes to be acceptable to him. This duty is precedent, both in order of time and in degree of obligation, to the claims of civil society. Before any man can be considered as a member of civil society, he must be considered as a subject of the Governor of the Universe . . .

James Madison

81

FREEDOM

"I WAS FREE"

Harriet Tubman (1820–1913) was an escaped slave who repeatedly risked her life to free slaves using the network of antislavery activists and safe houses known as the Underground Railroad. Also known as "Moses," Tubman was an African-American abolitionist who inspired generations of African-Americans struggling for equality and civil rights. During the Civil War she served as a Union spy, and after the war she helped set up schools for freed slaves and struggled for women's suffrage.

To her biographer, Sarah H. Bradford, Harriet Tubman stated:

> I had crossed de line of which I had so long been dreaming. I was free; but dere was no one to welcome me to de land of freedom, I was a stranger in a strange land, and my home after all was down in de old cabin quarter, wid de ole folks, and my brudders and sisters. But to dis solemn resolution I came; I was free, and dey should be free also; I would make a home for dem in de North, and de Lord helping me, I would bring dem all dere. Oh, how I prayed den, lying all alone on de cold, damp ground; "Oh, dear Lord," I said, "I haint got no friend but you. Come to my help, Lord, for I'm in trouble!"
>
> 'Twant me, 'twas the Lord. I always told Him, "I trust to You. I don't know where to go or what to do, but I expect You to lead me," and He always did.

Harriet Tubman

The General Principles of Liberty

In a letter to Thomas Jefferson on June 28, 1813, John Adams wrote:

The general principles, on which the Fathers achieved independence, were the only principles in which that beautiful assembly of young gentlemen could unite. . . . And what were these general principles? I answer, the general principles of Christianity, in which all these sects were united: And the general principles of English and American liberty, in which all those young men united, and which had united all parties in America, in majorities sufficient to assert and maintain her independence.

Now I will avow, that I then believe, and now believe, that those general principles of Christianity, are as eternal and immutable, as the existence and attributes of God; and that those principles of liberty, are as unalterable as human nature and our terrestrial, mundane system.

John Adams

83

MORAL STRENGTH

... and purify for Himself His own special people, zealous for good works.

TITUS 2:14

THE PURIFYING INFLUENCE OF CHRISTIANITY

Samuel Sullivan Cox (1824–1889) was a Congressman and U.S. Ambassador to the Ottoman Empire who stated in a Memorial address to Congress:

I believe in the religion which was taught and exemplified in the life of the Nazarene, and I never fail to bear testimony to the ennobling and purifying influence of the Christian religion. . . .

There was a poignancy in my heart when I saw the old church, where I so often worshipped, razed to the ground. Was it not there I attended my first Sunday school? There it was that I learned my Bible verses . . .

Those early memories were cut in durable stone. Tarnished by worldliness, dusted with the activities of life, they have pursued me through the various vicissitudes of professional, literary, and political life. They became the nucleus of studies in college; the very coat of mail in the struggles against selfishness and skepticism; in fine, they prefigured and preordained my choice of spiritual belief against the delusive sophistries of new philosophies and mere material science.

They have enabled me, in following and studying the physical advancement of the past century, to perceive in all the atoms, forms, and forces of nature and the phenomena of mind, the truth and benignity of the great scheme of human redemption, which is founded on the veracity of Christ, and becomes, with lapsing years, more beautiful with the white radiance of an ennobling spirituality.

Samuel Sullivan Cox

84

No Book Like the Bible

For we did not follow cunningly devised fables . . .

2 PETER 1:16

Charles Anderson Dana (1819–1897) was the editor-in-chief of the *New York Sun*, one of the largest newspapers in the country, and considered by many the most brilliant journalist in the country at that time. He wrote:

I believe in Christianity; that it is the religion taught to men by God Himself in person on earth. I also believe the Bible to be a Divine revelation. Christianity is not comparable with any other religion. It is the religion which came from God's own lips, and therefore the only true religion. The incarnation is a fact, and Christianity is based on revealed truth.

There are some books that are absolutely indispensable to the kind of education that we are contemplating, and to the profession that we are now considering; and of all these, the most indispensable, the most useful, the one whose knowledge is most effective, is the Bible. There is no Book from which more valuable lessons can be learned. I am considering it now as a manual of utility, or professional preparation, and professional use for a journalist.

There is no Book whose style is more suggestive and more instructive, from which you learn more directly that sublime simplicity which never exaggerates, which recounts the greatest event with solemnity, of course, but without sentimentality or affection, none which you open with such confidence and lay down with such reverence; there is no Book like the Bible.

Charles Anderson Dana

INSPIRING

"THE DESTINY OF AMERICA"

Calvin Coolidge, the 30th President of the United States (1923–1929), spoke on the motives of the Puritan forefathers in a message entitled "The Destiny of America":

If there be a destiny, it is of no avail to us unless we work with it. The ways of Providence will be of no advantage to us unless we proceed in the same direction. If we perceive a destiny in America, if we believe that Providence has been our guide, our own success, our own salvation requires that we should act and serve in harmony and obedience. ....

Settlers came here from mixed motives, some for pillage and adventure, some for trade and refuge, but those who have set their imperishable mark upon our institutions came from far higher motives. Generally defined, they were seeking a broader freedom. They were intent upon establishing a Christian commonwealth in accordance to the principle of self-government.

They were an inspired body of men. It has been said that God sifted the nations that He might send choice grain into the wilderness. They had a genius for organized society on the foundations of piety, righteousness, liberty, and obedience of the law. They brought with them the accumulated wisdom and experience of the ages. ... Who can fail to see in it the hand of destiny? Who can doubt that it has been guided by a Divine Providence?

Calvin Coolidge

86

The Haystack Prayer Meeting

In August 1806, five Williams College students met in a field for one of their twice-weekly prayer meetings, when a thunderstorm drove them to take refuge in a nearby haystack. Continuing in prayer, Samuel John Mills shared his burden that Christianity be sent abroad, and the group prayed that American missions would spread Christianity through the East. The Haystack Prayer Meeting held in Williamstown, Massachusetts, is viewed by many scholars as the spark that ignited American support for world missions for subsequent decades.

In 1808, the Haystack Prayer group and other Williams students formed "The Brethren," a society organized to "effect, in the persons of its members, a mission to the heathen." Within a few years, they inspired the founding of the American Board of Commissioners for Foreign Missions (ABCFM). Several of the students, including Adoniram Judson, went to Asia as missionaries (the first foreign missionaries sent from America in 1812), and Samuel Mills stayed stateside to recruit others and later helped organize the American Bible Society and the United Foreign Missionary Society.

In its first fifty years, the ABCFM sent out over 1,250 missionaries. In 1961, the American Board merged to form the United Church Board for World Missions (UCBWM). After 150 years, the American Board had sent out nearly 5,000 missionaries to 34 different fields, and it all began with five young men praying in a haystack.

"But there is a God in heaven who reveals secrets ..."

DANIEL 2:28

"THE GOD WHO MADE THE PEANUT"

George Washington Carver (1864–1943) was a fabulous chemist of international fame in the field of agriculture. Much of his fame was based on his research and promotion of alternative crops to soil-depleting cotton, such as the peanut, soybean, pecan, and sweet potato. He wanted poor farmers to grow alternative crops as both a source of their own food as well as a source of other products to improve their quality of life.

In 1921, Carver spoke in favor of a peanut tariff before the Ways and Means Committee of the United States House of Representatives. At the time, it was unusual for a black person to be called as an expert. He also detailed the potential uses of the peanut and other new crops to improve the economy of the South. At the end of his address, the Chairman of the Committee asked:

"Dr. Carver, how did you learn all of these things?"

Carver answered: "From an old book."

"What book?"

Carver replied, "The Bible."

The Senator inquired, "Does the Bible tell about peanuts?"

"No, sir," Dr. Carver replied, "but it tells about the God who made the peanut. I asked Him to show me what to do with the peanut, and He did."

George Washington Carver

THE PUREST MORALITY

MORAL STRENGTH

Benjamin Franklin Butler (1795–1858), a lawyer who served as the U.S. Attorney General under President Andrew Jackson (1833–1838), stated:

He is truly happy, whatever may be his temporal condition, who can call God his Father in the full assurance of faith and hope. And amid all his trials, conflicts, and doubts, the feeblest Christian is still comparatively happy; because cheered by the hope . . . that the hour is coming when he shall be delivered from "this body of sin and death" and in the vision of his Redeemer . . . approximate to the . . . felicity of angels.

Not only does the Bible inculcate, with sanctions of the highest import, a system of the purest morality, but in the person and character of our Blessed Savior it exhibits a tangible illustration of that system.

In Him we have set before us—what, till the publication of the Gospel, the world had never seen—a model of feeling and action, adapted to all times, places, and circumstances; and combining so much of wisdom, benevolence, and holiness, that none can fathom its sublimity; and yet, presented in a form so simple, that even a child may be made to understand and taught to love it.

Benjamin Franklin Butler

TRUTH

"*No one comes to the Father except through Me.*"

JOHN 14:6

NO ORDINARY CLAIMS

Simon Greenleaf (1783–1853) was the Royall Professor of Law at Harvard and considered one of the greatest legal minds in Western history. In his *Testimony of the Evangelists*, Greenleaf stated:

The religion of Jesus Christ aims at nothing less than the utter overthrow of all other systems of religion in the world; denouncing them as inadequate to the wants of man, false in their foundations, and dangerous in their tendency. It not only solicits the grave attention of all, to whom its doctrines are presented, but it demands their cordial belief, as a matter of vital concernment.

These are no ordinary claims; and it seems hardly possible for a rational being to regard them with even a subdued interest; much less to treat them with mere indifference and contempt. If not true, they are little else than the pretensions of a bold imposture, which, not satisfied with having already enslaved millions of the human race, seeks to continue its encroachments upon human liberty, until all nations shall be subjugated under its iron rule.

But if they are well-founded and just, they can be no less than the high requirements of heaven, addressed by the voice of God to the reason and understanding of man, concerning things deeply affecting his relations to his sovereign, and essential to the formation of his character and of course to his destiny, both for this life and for the life to come.

Simon Greenleaf

RELIGION SUPPORTS THE STATE

Robert Winthrop, a lawyer and philanthropist who served as the Speaker of the United States House of Representatives (1847–1849), stated:

The voice of experience and the voice of our own reason speak but one language. . . . Both united in teaching us that men may as well build their houses upon the sand and expect to see them stand, when the rains fall, and the winds blow, and the floods come, as to found free institutions upon any other basis than that of morality and virtue, of which the Word of God is the only authoritative rule, and the only adequate sanction.

All societies of men must be governed in some way or other. The less they have of stringent state government, the more they must have of individual self-government. The less they rely on public law or physical force, the more they must rely on private moral restraint.

Men, in a word, must necessarily be controlled either by a power within them or a power without them; either by the Word of God or by the strong arm of man; either by the Bible or by the bayonet.

It may do for other countries and other governments to talk about the state supporting religion. Here, under our own free institutions, it is religion which must support the state.

Robert Winthrop

91

"The Battle Hymn of the Republic"

IN NOVEMBER 1861, after a visit to a Union Army camp, Julia Ward Howe wrote the poem that came to be called "The Battle Hymn of the Republic." It became the best-known Civil War song of the Union Army as well as a well-loved American patriotic anthem.

Mine eyes have seen the glory of the coming of the Lord:
He is trampling out the vintage where the grapes of wrath are
 stored;
He hath loosed the fateful lightning of His terrible swift sword:
His truth is marching on.

I have seen Him in the watch-fires of a hundred circling camps,
They have builded Him an altar in the evening dews and
 damps;
I can read His righteous sentence by the dim and
 flaring lamps:
His day is marching on.

I have read a fiery gospel writ in burnished
 rows of steel:
"As ye deal with my contemners, so with
 you my grace shall deal;
Let the Hero, born of woman, crush the
 serpent with His heel,
Since God is marching on."

He has sounded forth the trumpet that
 shall never call retreat;
He is sifting out the hearts of men before
 His judgment-seat:
Oh, be swift, my soul, to answer Him! be
 jubilant, my feet!
Our God is marching on.

In the beauty of the lilies Christ was
 born across the sea,
With a glory in His bosom that
 transfigures you and me:
As He died to make men holy, let us die
 to make men free,
While God is marching on.

93

"My Country, 'Tis of Thee"

SAMUEL FRANCIS SMITH wrote the words to "My Country, 'Tis of Thee," also known as "America," while studying at Andover Theological Seminary in 1831. The song's inspirational words are matched with a popular international melody used by many nations, including England, where it accompanies "God Save the King/Queen." The hymn soon became a national favorite, serving as a de facto national anthem of the United States for much of the nineteenth century.

My country, 'tis of thee, sweet land of liberty, of thee I sing:
Land where my fathers died, land of the pilgrims' pride,
From every mountainside let freedom ring!

My native country, thee, land of the noble free, thy name I love:
I love thy rocks and rills, thy woods and templed hills;
My heart with rapture thrills, like that above.

Let music swell the breeze, and ring from
*   all the trees sweet freedom's song:*
Let mortal tongues awake; let all that
*   breathe partake;*
Let rocks their silence break, the sound
*   prolong.*

Our fathers' God, to Thee, author of
*   liberty, to Thee we sing:*
Long may our land be bright
*   with freedom's holy light.*
Protect us by Thy might,
*   great God, our King!*

Photo & Illustration Credits

• **1** John Trumbull • **2-3** ©2008 Jupiterimages Corporation • **4** Courtesy Ronald Reagan Library | Library of Congress • **7** ©2008 Jupiterimages Corporation • **8-9** ©2008 Jupiterimages Corporation • **10-11** www.historywiz.com | www.freepages.genealogy.rootsweb.ancestry.com • **12** ©2008 Jupiterimages Corporation • **15** National Park Service • **16-17** ©2008 Jupiterimages Corporation • **18** Robert W. Weir • **19** ©2008 Jupiterimages Corporation • **20** Al Aumuller • **21** NASA • **22** Thomas Le Mere • **23** NASA • **24** Auguste Millière • **25** JJstroker (Wikimedia Commons) • **26** Paulos (Wikimedia Commons) • **27** Janneman (Wikimedia Commons) • **28** Gilbert Stuart • **29** Robert Aitken • **30** Library of Congress • **31** White House Press Office • **32** Donna Miles • **33** SrA Tana R. Hamilton • **34** Chester Harding • **35** Craig Sowell (www.findagrave.com) • **36** Gerald L. Nino • **37** Courtesy of the Senator John Heinz History Center • **38** Library of Congress • **39** Jlorenz1 (Wikimedia Commons) • **40** Courtesy Ronald Reagan Library • **41** Sarony & Major, 1846 • **42** Henry S. Sadd • **43** James Peale • **44** Library of Congress • **45** Department of Defense • **46** Sclchua (Wikimedia Commons) • **47** Kelson (Wikimedia Commons) • **48** Executive Office of the President of the United States • **49** Eric Draper • **50** Executive Office of the President of the United States • **51** Library of Congress • **52** John Blake White • **53** ©2008 Jupiterimages Corporation • **54** Library of Congress • **55** John. H. Bufford • **56** NASA • **57** United States Department of Agriculture • **58** Ragesoss (Wikimedia Commons) • **59** Library of Congress • **60** John Singleton Copley • **61** Scribner & Co. • **62** United States Federal Government • **63** D.M. Carter and A.H. Ritchie • **64** Sarony & Major • **65** Library of Congress • **66** Jed (Wikimedia Commons) • **67** Mike Cline (Wikimedia Commons) • **69** Abbie Rowe, National Park Service • **70** Currier & Ives • **71** John Rous • **72** Samuel King • **74** Eric Draper, Executive Office of the President of the United States • **75** ©2008 Jupiterimages Corporation • **76** Library of Congress • **77** Warren K. Leffler • **78** George P.A. Healy • **79** National Park Service, U.S. Department of the Interior • **80** Henry R. Robinson • **81** Pendleton's Lithography • **82** H.B. Lindsley • **83** Library of Congress • **84** Library of Congress • **85** Mathew Brady • **86** Notman Photo Co., Boston, Mass • **87** Daderot (Wikimedia Commons) • **88** Frances Benjamin Johnston • **89** *The Bay State Monthly*, Volume I. No. VI. June, 1884 • **90** Adam sk (Wikimedia Commons) • **91** Mathew Brady • **92** Kurz & Allison • **93** Gerlach-Barklow Co. • **94** ©2008 Jupiterimages Corporation | Library of Congress

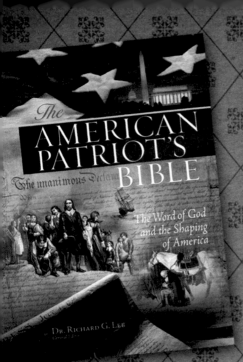

Discover.

Experience.

Examine.

THE WORD OF GOD AN[D]
THE SHAPING OF AMERI[CA]

THE AMERICAN PATRIOT'S BIBLE
connects the teachings of the Bible with
the history of the Unites States while
applying it to today's culture. Beautiful
full-color insert pages spotlight
America's greatest thinkers, leaders,
and events that present the rich heri-
tage and future of our great nation.

Sometimes history does repeat itself.